GOD

GOD

Debora Greger

Penguin Poets

PENGUIN BOOKS

Published by the Penguin Group

Penguin Putnam Inc., 375 Hudson Street,
New York, New York 10014, U.S.A.
Penguin Books Ltd, 27 Wrights Lane,
London W8 5TZ, England
Penguin Books Australia Ltd, Ringwood,
Victoria, Australia
Penguin Books Canada Ltd, 10 Alcorn Avenue,
Toronto, Ontario, Canada M4V 3B2
Penguin Books (N.Z.) Ltd, 182–190 Wairau Road,
Auckland 10, New Zealand

Penguin Books Ltd, Registered Offices:
Harmondsworth, Middlesex, England

First published in Penguin Books 2001

10 9 8 7 6 5 4 3 2 1

Copyright © Debora Greger, 2001
All rights reserved

Page vi constitutes an extension of this copyright page.

ISBN 14 04.2433 4
CIP data available

Printed in the United States of America
Set in Walbaum
Designed by Soonyoung Kwon

for George and Zara Steiner

Acknowledgments

Antioch Review: "The Porcupine," "The Ruined Abbey"
Gettysburg Review: "British Rail," "The Civil War," "Subtropical Elegy"
The Nation: "There Now"
The New England Review: "God in Florida," "Head, Perhaps of an Angel"
The New Republic: "The Dead of Summer," "A Property of the National Trust"
Paris Review: "Moss in the Hamptons, "To the Snow"
Partisan Review: "The Laurel Tree by the River"
Ploughshares: "The Snow Leopard"
Poetry: "The British Museum," "Easter 1991," "Eve at the Paradise," "The Feast of Thomas Becket" (as "Les Très Riches Heures de Paris"), "The Twilight of England"
Salmagundi: "Admiral of the Parking Lot," "The Allotment Garden," "The Eden of Florida," "Persephone in the Underworld," "To a Blackbird," "Variante de la Tristesse: The Sadness of the Subtropics"
Western Humanities Review: "Miranda on the British Isles"
Yale Review: "The Overland Bus"

"Memoirs of a Saint" was first published in *Lines/Lignes: Réflexions/Reflections* (UCLA, 1996)

on the cover: Wampum Snake and Red Lily, from *The Natural History of Carolina, Florida, and the Bahamas* by Mark Catesby, 1771 (Department of Special Collections, George A. Smathers Libraries, University of Florida)

The poor maidservant who used to say that she only believed in God when she had a toothache puts all theologians to shame.

—E. M. CIORAN

Contents

God in Florida

Q. *Who created the heavens and the earth?*
A. *God.*
Q. *How long was God in creating all things?*
A. *Six days.*
Q. *What did God create on the first day?*
A. *Light.*
Q. *What was created on the second day?*
A. *The firmament.*
Q. *What the third?*
A. *Vegetables.*

—*Child's Scripture Question Book,* 1879

Book I: Pseudepigrapha
I Was Alone,

God said,
And out of loneliness
thought to make someone

who could tell me a story.
There was nothing but water in the dark.
That was the first day.

And so on.
Stars dragging themselves
out of the wet to dry,

but I needed better light.
I needed dirt.
There went a third day, and a fourth.

And in the vast emptiness
I tried stocking the bodies of water.
Like a face newly coined,

something glinted in the deep.
That was the fifth day,
but it wasn't enough.

And by the sixth day already
there was dust on everything.
I swept it up.

Out of my own dust I made someone.
I should have retired.
I should have gone fishing instead.

In the Beginning Was the Worm,

God said, And the worm was without a god.
The worm was a god.
Cities fell, a foot or more,

because of him. No one was buried
but he ate the first clod.
And men shone a light in the dark

and dug into the deep,
and the nightcrawler crawled out.
And I, their god, wriggled on the hook.

The God of Alligators

said, "Lie down.
I can think only lying down.
Eternity is easier to take that way.

You don't have to make dry land
till mating season starts.
Then men will say

they saw you crossing the road
to the International House of Pancakes
south of town,

though you're interested only
in the female bellowing at you
from the deeps beyond."

Old Red-Eye, God said,
What would I know about finding a mate?
I just like to look

on all that I have made,
whether insects mating
or the British talking.

I, the retired god,
watch public television much of the evening,
and go south in the winter.

The Third Day,

give or take
a few million years,
the first blade of grass appeared.

And God said,
I have confounded Darwin—
the man wants to know

how it happened so fast.
Redbird, look at his curious beak.
Pass him a seed, cardinal—

no, the man wants flesh.
See how he fluffs his tailcoat,
preens and struts?

And on the fourth day,
in the hotel bar at Disney World,
God said, What would I know

about sexual selection?
Though I put on the hat of the Mouse,
the ears mean nothing to me.

And it was evening,
and it was morning,
the fifth day.

Dinosaurs tore at the darkness,
doomed as prophets. And God said,
I am like unto the leathery bird

with nowhere to go,
who flaps like a wallet
over the swamp primeval.

How could I be dying,
who love the smell of mildew
in the morning?

Book II: The Retired God in the New World

I don't like the man who doesn't sleep, says God . . .
Sleep is perhaps the most beautiful thing I have created.
And I myself rested on the seventh day.   —PÉGUY

The Seventh Day,

God said, I longed to take my rest
like any animal.
Sunday after lunch, the creatures fed—

it was siesta time at the Paradise Zoo.
Along the thin arm of a branch,
the lemur cradled itself in sleep

as if, should it slip,
angels like apes would bear it up.
The seraphic snowy owl,

pinions pinned, wing yet to mend,
took and ate of the mouse.
Only the alligator was hard at work,

a god, flopped on a mudbank,
who winked the world's slowest wink.
A lesser egret tiptoed by,

a Sunday hat on its way to church.
I yawned, God said. And when I woke
it was the eighth day.

A man was naming the animals.
A name hung on each cage.
Flinging themselves down

like angels, the gibbons spoke
only in their own tongue now.
I waited to be called by name.

I rolled over and played dead.

The Seventh Night,

God said, I can't sleep
with all the racket.
The cricket and the frog—

why do they keep singing,
who have no mate in which to rejoice?
O bookworm boring your way

through my collected works, read on!
Did you recognize me?
Am I their god?

The cockroach would not enter my words
but devoted himself to the binding,
devouring the ancient starch.

On the old card catalogue,
shoved into the corner, no longer used,
the *Niña* sagged against the *Santa Maria*

like the whores of Castile
whose names they bore.
O Eves of easy virtue,

the cardboard seas are rough
with dust, the *Pinta* long since lost
to the night janitor's mop.

Ladies, I can't sleep. Write down the words
they put in my mouth,
my ration of bread and water.

Don't forget to use quotation marks.
Do it the way the priests do.
In the beginning. At the end.

The Fourth Month,

God said,
The men made landfall at last,
and fell to their knees on the beach,

shouting, "For God, for God and spices."
As if the sand, so white,
the palms, so royal, could understand.

And in the fifth month,
their priest translated the *Confessionario*
into the local dialect.

The tribe watched the priest break the bread
and mutter to it, his back to them.
And still they watched

to see if, as he claimed,
the bread became a god.
He ate his god.

And the worm crawled through the village
like a missionary, drew near
to learn their word for paradise

and found it dirty, knowing only dirt.

Lamentation over the Suwannee

I, the retired God, swore
and threaded a new worm on the hook.
Across the face of the deep I cast,

not even snagging my own reflection.
Along the shore of the lake
the smell of lighter fluid drifted.

Whose lost harps hung in the willows?
Brother Bartolomé, put down your ghost quill.
The dead king still does not believe

all that you say De Soto did.
Is that your scribble on the water
or the wind's chapter and verse?

The osprey swoops low like a god,
watching for movement in the water.
Lesser egret, what good is regret?

My right hand withers,
my tongue clings to the roof of my mouth.
I winter in Florida.

Book III: Acts of the Retired God

What would be left of our tragedies if a literate insect were to present us his?

Grace before Meals

Don't interrupt me, God said.
I may be an old god
in the rainy season,

being read to by a mockingbird,
waiting for the rain to stop—
but one for whom the Spaniards fought.

In the warm rain,
knee-deep in water lilies,
bitten under the armor

by the mosquitoes, malarial,
that drove the natives deeper
into the lilies of the lake.

Mock-bird, it's time for our catechism.
Can all land creatures swim?
Most land-dwellers can if they have to.

And consider the water-strider.
Yes, I want to hear the part
where the famous scientist admits

all that can be known of God is
he has an inordinate fondness
for beetles. Bird, you and I both.

Do I hear myself called to dinner?
Did they not say my name,
saying grace? Or was it you, mocker?

After-Dinner Grace

The dead poet squatted on the windowsill,
monkish, feeding on crumbs,
a good cockroach in the dark.

Under the flowering judas,
by the sweet cross
of the New World passionflower,

the sainted roach, convert,
slurred the Jews for his art.
Where was the mantis to pray

like the pound sign
over the insect once a bank clerk?
Let the dead feed on the dead.

After such forgiveness, what?
An after-dinner nap?
Do I stiffen in a new house,

I, an old god borne by the trade winds
to a golf-course condominium?
Stay awake, songbird. Read me the part

where the scientist says
how like a virus is religion:
an outbreak leaves a lot of them dead.

Religion has many cunning passages.
You could get lost on your way to bed.
Let the dead sleep. For the dead.

Lamentation over the Fountain of Youth

Do they still take my name in vain
at the sand trap or the water hazard
of the Fountain of Youth Golf Course?

Or was it just you, mockingbird?
But, no, you sing of the forbidden fruit
of the gallberry, the cabbage palm.

How can you eat such stuff?
O gray bird, state bird of paradise!
Sing the old prophets, like Milton's daughters.

Out of his blindness, he makes them
pronounce the Aramaic perfectly.
Only he need know what it means.

Two birds of drabbest plume before him drove . . .
How like you the dead poet,
who sings until we're dry, and then sings on.

I, the old desert god, say,
Pass him a grub.
He shares your appetite for fame.

O my little gray Puritan, sing that line again.
That Heav'n would want spectators,
God want praise—I like that, out of context.

In the Garden,

I should have dug the ha-ha deeper,
God said, To keep them in.
In the end

there was only one gardener
I was jealous of.
"I have so much to do," he wrote.

"When I am galloping off
in one part of the world,
my men are making blunders in another."

There was earth to be moved
to make nature look natural.
There were, across the water

in the second distance
that was the empire,
rebellious colonies in the new Eden.

And so Capability Brown—
who would let his clients plant
only the most English of trees—

rode between the garden of the statesman,
who pled for the colonies,
and the garden of the king.

And when Brown died,
the king said to the gardener's assistant,
"Now you and I can do here what we please."

Past the ha-ha
dug to keep the deer
from the great house,

past the paradise garden
now fallen from favor,
over the ocean, past the folly,

past the ghost slave ship
and the ship of cotton shroud,
while the king's plant hunter crouched low,

forced to devour his sample seeds,
I, an old god in the New World,
envied the king.

Book IV: The Revelations of Florida

The greatest piece of good luck Jesus had was that He died young. Had He lived to be sixty, He would have given us His memoirs instead of the cross.

—CIORAN

In the Presence of Cardinals

They scatter before me:
down the walk the anoles bow and scrape.
I could get used to this, God said,

If I were just a man. Don't tell me
that Emerson was right.
If a man is a god in ruins,

not an animal, then I am
just a mirror walking down the road,
past the white cemetery.

They hoard their dead in the ground.
After the rain they bring plastic flowers
and a red toy telephone

bearing the words "Jesus called."
What do they want me to say, cardinal?
You—you love to do the "whip, whip, whip!"

that is your cry alone.
And then there you are, neck snapped,
a little fistful of blood-colored feathers,

who fell for your own reflection
in the plate glass
of Allmighty G Bail Bonds.

And Another Thing,

God said.
On the fourth Sunday of Advent,
in the church of the oil baron

in St. Augustine, they sang the *Messiah*
at cruising speed. Gone the recitatives.
Gone the one whom you seek,

before you even notice—
I, *deus absconditus,*
gone down the street:

at Ripley's *Believe It or Not!*
they worship the golden six-legged calf.
Prepare ye the way.

Make straight a highway down the beach.
December, let's go. It's time to head south
like the robins. Drunk on fire-thorn berries,

they splash in the streets
where Hell's Angels slouch
toward Daytona to be reborn.

The Second Coming

To the gopher tortoise
God said, O conquistador's helmet
to which the jungle laid claim!

O soup tureen of some lost colony, overturned!
The possum laid out in death
on the shoulder would show us how

to cross four lanes of traffic.
Take my son with you.
He is small enough,

the god of the dashboard,
the *imprimatur* of Taiwan on his foot.
The magnet won't hold his feet to your shell.

To the tortoise who would enter Paradise,
God said, Wait for the light to change
at the corner of De Soto and Main.

A Tropical Depression

As it happens, God said,
I'm tired of being a god.
It happens that I can't sleep

with a woodpecker knocking at the house.
Who does he think he is, called the lord god?
Let him find his termites somewhere else.

I, the voice in the whirlwind, open the door—
and someone's cat has left a headless rat
on the front walk. I should be moved

by such an offering—the gods always are.
I should be among the dead.
The smell of wet leaves burning

at a makeshift funeral pyre—
I want to cry out. Oh, what manure!
I want to crawl under the mold.

I, a dung beetle who spent the day
rolling a ball of dung across the sky,
which is to say, a god. Let there be dark.

Book V: Apocrypha

I don't have to live in New York. I could live in hell.

The End of History

I speak in the only voice left me,
God said, That of an old star
light years away, half dead,

though you wouldn't know it.
A woman in dark glasses. A crank.
I don't have to live in Florida,

I could live in a condo in hell.
I want to be alone in the movie theater.
Cockroach, stop chewing:

Garbo dies for my sins.
She coughs her way to heaven,
tart with a rusty heart, then rises again.

She sweeps in like Eve,
she swears like the Virgin Mary.
In the paradise of Paris, she laughs,

a Marxist about to fall from grace,
in love with a farcical hat.
I love Brother Marx,

who was right about one thing.
I'm better the second time,
all that tragedy made farce.

The Eighth Day,

God said, When they came to me
and said, "You are a *god*,"
I felt sick.

And on the ninth day,
when they came to me and said it again,
I thought, "They exaggerate."

And on the tenth day,
when they said, "You *are* God,"
I managed to thank them.

And on the eleventh day,
when I looked on all that I had made,
I saw it wasn't that bad.

And on the twelfth day,
when I looked on myself in the mirror,
I thought, "I am who I am."

And on the thirteenth day,
I asked why I hadn't killed myself
the day before.

In the End

Another Saturday night in hell,
God said. No lost city of gold,
and now in my name

the Knights of Columbus
exact their tribute on Bingo night,
in the old movie theater.

O Easter vigil! G 3! O 33!
Into the dark the voice is carried.
Into the cave

of a lily's long white throat,
a late worker bee has stumbled,
refusing to rise.

As out of a winter sweater,
the chameleon god shrugged off its skin
and ate. This is my body.

I am what I cling to, bark or leaf.
Seething is believing.
I flicked my long tongue experimentally—

the world stuck to my word.
To show myself,
I puffed out the red fan of my throat

to draw you close, to scare you off.
Draw nigh unto me with your mouth.
Honor me with your lips.

Tell this old god one last story.
Start at the beginning
and make it good.

The next Augustan age will dawn on the other side of the Atlantic. There will, perhaps, be a Thucydides at Boston, a Xenophon at New York, and, in time, a Virgil at Mexico, and a Newton at Peru. At last, some curious traveler from Lima will visit England and give a description of the ruins of St. Paul's, like the editions of Balbec and Palmyra.

—WALPOLE

Easter 1991

All changed, changed utterly:
A terrible beauty is born.
                    —YEATS

Something has rolled from its cave
          and under the fence
of the Botanic Garden, onto the sidewalk:
          a handful of thorns,
their hour come and gone, a hedgehog half-risen,
          dead leaves cast off—
see the place where it lay in the underbrush,
          a sleepy grenade?
Now it drowses in the open, back from the dead
          of English winter,
stunned by the dizzying half-warm sun.
          The stone rolled away.
Two men all in white stood by the tomb—

          if I've seen them,
I haven't known them for what they were,
          young men from the next island
passing for young men here, the gray ones
          down on their luck, perhaps,
who've eked enough for a pint and a game
          of darts at the local pub.
Somewhere, in a potting shed, something waits
          to be transformed utterly—
bags of fertilizer, lengths of pipe—
          into a homemade bomb.
A briefcase left at a railway station,
          a pane of glass

sent flying by the blast, a shattered rain
    on the chosen "soft target"—
this is the beauty of terror, the glass
    in the midst of all
the terrorist knows, who calls the radio station
    from Her Majesty's pay phone.
Minute by minute a timer ticks
    for ambushed husband,
gun-running priest. *Why do you seek the living*
    among the dead? Come see
the place where he lay, then go quickly.
    Do not be terrified.

Rough beast that bristled at the suggestion
    that it move—
for its thorns we cast lots.
    It played dead,
rolled into a ball you rolled under the fence
    back into winter,
your palm pierced for your trouble.
    We have bowed
at its feet, the leathery dark
    of the dead.
We could not number all its spines.

The British Museum
The Portland Vase

It was just a Roman translation, too flowery,
     of some long-lost Greek,
but still I stood in front of the vase
     Keats had stood before,
waiting to feel what he felt then,
     or later, on paper—
I wasn't particular. I wasn't

     even a scholar, heartbroken,
forced to admit, at least in a footnote,
     that she couldn't prove
on which vase, exactly, Keats had seen
     that heifer lowing at the skies.
And what green altar, O mysterious priest?
     Where was the sacrifice?

A milky goddess held a milk-white snake
     almost to her breast—
was this what she wanted Keats to see?
     He'd read medicine—
when the lungs wasted with each bloody breath,
     the barber-surgeon was sent for,
who ministered the blessed leech.

     Cold pastoral! For ever warm . . .
He stood before a blacksmith's shop,
     longing for a fire,
on the long walk home. *For ever panting,*
     and for ever young—

he was just twenty-three. There would be time
        for South America,

he would sign as surgeon on an Indiaman,
        spend a year in Kentucky
if it were near a library.
        A burning forehead,
and a parching tongue—he knew the symptoms,
        and wrote them off
to lovesickness a few months longer.

The Elgin Marbles

So much smaller than I expected,
    the old operating theater
intimate—the only word that could be applied,
    like a compress,
to the open wound of a room.
    Even the squeamish
in the top row at the back, the dreamy,

    the teenage Keats,
doodling instead of taking notes,
    could have seen the child smile
at the doctor, who burst into tears,
    the operation proceeding—
once the patient had been blindfolded—
    without anesthetic.

The stains ingrained in the floor,
    the hacksaws polished,
the scars homely in the crude table,
    an apron hung up
to wait like good meat for the butcher,
    a box of sawdust
left to catch the blood—

    flesh was just marble.
The goddess of domestic life,
    whose arms were stumps,
had lost her head to some argument,
    brutal or trivial,

no one remembered now. His mother dead
these seven years.

His brother's cough. The river god,
waked by some noise,
who raised himself on one perfect arm
to see what had happened,
was missing both his hands and feet.
The horse was just a head,
the stone still quivering with fatigue.

To a Blackbird

I

See how the young blackbird
    quivers and mewls,
trailing its darker, unruffled father
    across the treacherous lawn—

see, the adult has halted, head cocked,
    as if to impart a lesson
in how best not to listen to the young
    who feign hurt just to be fed:

you pay him no mind. This is an art,
    the way you listen
for something not there—a worm
    turning the earth,

the worm you tear in two in play.
    Gold-beaked Solomon,
in all dirts wise—for the young's own good,
    you swallow the worm whole.

You turn your sleek ministerial tail.
    You listen for nothing.
"Already I feel my loneliness a little,"
    Rilke has written to his wife,

"and suspect it will refuse me nothing.
    Are you not the one tree,
dear distance, I sometimes look back on?
    This brazen beak shrieks

at you: Don't come, don't come!"

2

How the blackbird pours out his song
    like milk spilling
over the unbuttoned elderflower,
    over the bed gone wild,

misty-eyed love-in-a-mist so clearly
    strayed from its border.
Bird, you are just like Rilke.
    You turn your glossy back.

You parade and strut the grounds
    of a titled lady
and then retire to compose a letter
    to wife and daughter:

"Sometimes I wake up in the night,
    something calling,
calling the dark valley down below.
    The sweet mounting voice

that never ceases to mount—
    had it hands and face?
An entire being changed into a voice—
    never has silence gone

to such great lengths to bare its loss.
    Slowly I draw it
into my room, past my bed,
    and into me.

39

Now there is nothing but shadow
        on the upper terraces
where the frock of a girl shimmers
        more mysteriously.

The park, split by the wail of the last train,
        shows its insides
like a burst fruit, withered and moldy.
        The night wind

has caught on the soul of some animal."

Miranda on the British Isles

Were I in England now, as I once was, and had but this fish painted, not a holiday fool there but would give a piece of silver: there would this monster make a man; any strange beast there makes a man; when they will not give a doit to relieve a lame beggar, they will lay out ten to see a dead Indian.

—The Tempest

Gray the rabbit pulled from the old hat,
gray the silk handkerchief and the dove.
Gray the rain on the seaside towns
that Prospero and Daughter played,

our magic to be taken with a grain of sand.
Still, there were always volunteers,
foreign sailors, out of their depth,
dying to be sawn in half in front of their mates

or the girl of the evening.
Sometimes, up to his neck in the trick cabinet,
well-worn patter heaped upon his well-lit head,
one winked at me. My father fretted,

the old saw threatening to give.
Gray the tempests pulled from teapots,
gray the mirrors and the smoke.
Below the trapdoor, waves slapped the pier

until it shuddered but held.
A teakettle shrieked backstage.
A foghorn moaned,
constant in its low complaint.

Oh, winch the curtains shut
on Old Asperity and Daughter!
A half-full house of flounder
rolled their eyes toward the wings,

where chorus girls saluted each other
for practice. The way sound carried over water,
I heard scales taken like stairs
in gray hotels where the lift was always out.

Walls made of paper, walls made of rain—
some nights next door a boat creaked over swells
and muddy from that woozy bed
came birdlike cries, then a beached groan.

My father and a chorus girl?
Old Bosporus? Did I want to know?
Like any fisherman at the nightly haul,
I had net to mend: my tights.

Nightly I played the native,
hoisting a cup of Earl Grey's bilge
to the wallpaper's gray roses.
Rain lashed the sea of gray slate roofs.

British Rail

In thy faint slumbers I by thee have watched
                                        —Henry IV, Part I

But soft, Shakespeare has put her to sleep,
the book laid open in her lap,
the pen no mightier than a sword

laid down between the lines,
drawn in her unshaken schoolgirl's hand,
that furrow the page:

the land is burning,
someone named Percy stands somewhere on high,
and either she or they must lower lie.

Through fields afire with rape in bloom,
the train bears a ragged, well-lagered handful
of soccer fans to battle,

ripe metal sullen on sodden ground.
The fat one wants to know
can honor take away the grief of a wound?

Away from the train, back into history,
farther back, all England races—
we have it backward, the scarecrow knows.

King against crows, puppet king,
he lifts his lord the farmer's empty sleeve
to greet death emptyhanded.

Can honor set a leg?
Dreamer, look to the highest field:
two pages of fresh-turned earth is room enough.

Such lullabies the scarecrow knows.
Lie down, lay thine ear close to the ground,
and list if thou canst hear the tread of travelers.

They rise from dust as if from sleep.

The Ruined Abbey
Single Panel from an Altarpiece

St. Joseph is about to gouge his thumb,
as if from his workbench he's heard the wings
of the angel who's appeared in the living room,
though only the pages of a book are quivering.
A lily leans toward the unexpected guest
to ask why, to leave the earth, you need all that clothing.
The Virgin ignores them, but you can guess the rest:
Joseph asking what happened and being told, "Nothing."

He's making a mousetrap though there's as yet no mouse.
The gown of the Virgin's bluer than the sky
at the little window, half-shuttered at the back of the house,
as if, her nose in a book, she's far away
from the symbols that clutter her fifteenth-century room.
Somewhere a stone rolls back from an empty tomb.

Single Leaf

But later what would the wise men say they saw?
A stable that smelled of straw and dung? A common
stable, a baby who looked old the way that human
babies do so that we'll hold them, in awe
of all they can't yet do, their only flaw—
would the wise men say they saw an omen?
Or just a man off to the side, asleep, a woman
who admitted the child wasn't his exactly. Ah . . .

but for now, in the miniature, they're all
dressed up, just waiting for something to happen,
making their way on horseback through a world
where a star just leads to another castle, the small
roofs blue as the woman's gown, the deep sky open,
empty, waiting for nothing to be unfurled.

The Feast of Thomas Becket

But in the book of hours it's still December,
as if someone forgot to unlock the case
and turn the page to what will happen after
the hunt that's rendered there, the clearing chaste
in the detail so loved by the luminous master:
the dogs that gore the stag, the same white as the cloud
of castle past the winter woods, past a
huntsman who calls the kill to the breathless world—

but through the window it's all but January.
There's the walled herb garden, a few brave stalks.
The sluggish Ouse, the barren orangery.
Only a starling scrounges along the walk
in its old Advent vestments, into the wind.
Only a jet breaks through the cloud to land.

The Allotment Garden

Under a flag of leaf now tattered,
    a giant marrow fattened
till none would touch it, old warhead.

    Only an insurgent slug
bored deeper into the pale, papery flesh
    until there was nothing to spy:

a bed of earth, cleared long ago,
    lay sealed at the border
by bramble's luxuriant barbed wire.

    On each green coil
where a wasp had raided, blackberries bled.
    A single poppy

had volunteered, but for what?
    The bright gash of petals
had been left to close itself for the night.

    A few radishes straggled,
Redcoats lost, out of formation.
    A lance of rhubarb

pierced the leaf smoke, and still it advanced.
    Who would tie it to the stake?
Only rainwater stood to attention

        in a tipsy watering can,
so still the surface bloomed with scum,
        a late imperious legion.

Knighting whatever it crawled past,
        the sun withdrew.
Each blade gleamed where it bent,

        unmoved, the underside
already dark. Hereward the Wake slept
        under his blanket of rust.

The Twilight of England
Summer

Late in the day, late in the century
a swan, which was to say, Her Majesty's by right,
rolled onto its side midstream and capsized.
It washed its wing whiter in the blackened river.

The codling worm had curled in the apple's heart,
the air grown rich on last year's leafy rot.
If the plum was a planet,
it was twilight on both sides,

the light worn out, the sun refusing to set
on the snail that conquered the windowpane,
trailing a slimy glitter.
A boy laid his head down on his Latin,

Tacitus still saying of this island,
one must remember we are dealing with barbarians
not yet softened by protracted peace.
Tacitus the emperor's son-in-law,

destined for the Colonial Service—
I do him a disservice who said
a bath and a good meal were enslavement,
vices as agreeable to the conquered

as to their conquerors.
The peonies, the pale blood-flecked ones,
laid down their heavy heads in the dirt.
Time for the last prayer

of the day to rise from the church
turned into a mosque, into the air
whose acid etched the stone
in a scabrous language no one spoke.

Time for the Curry Queen to open its doors,
the Imperial Boat to fry the first fish and chips,
next door to the Blackamoor's Head,
where the first pint of bitter had been drawn.

Winter

The feathers glittered by streetlight
like the new money minted, shrunken, from the old,
only Her Majesty's profile plumper,
the sun coined as weak as the pound.

In the butcher's window pheasants hung head down,
shot last weekend on the Queen's winter estate.
In the new Dark Ages the darkened mills
stood their sad ground, satanically cold.

This was the ruin of Britain,
the late prophet Gildas howled,
who got his dates wrong, his history tearful,
his sentence swollen with the splendors

of complaint. Who said, "I need say no more,"
and drew breath midstream.
Time for a rat to be elevated like the host
in the claws of the risen tawny owl.

For the wind to whine, unrepentant,
through the ruined abbey. To wrap its sheet
round the bones of the Knights Templar
who survived their holy desert war

only to be rowed through the pestilential mist
to an island abloom with ague and damp.
To lay themselves down forever.
To be picked clean by the holy lower orders.

A Property of the National Trust

We brought up the rear, the army recruiter and I.
Ghostly bulwarks of white cattle stood their ground.
In the sensible shoes I'd borrowed,
I picked my way through a no man's land

of pasture spiked with poppies.
Where chimney swifts banked and dove,
no gnat was safe in the twilight of England.
On wild mustard a gaseous ground-mist hung.

On the continent, what passed for peace
late in that century threatened to hold,
though somewhere far off. Neighbors still warred
in the old ways, house to house.

What was fifty years to a war?
Nothing to the great gardener,
who loved a beech tree most of all.
He could make England look natural

just by moving a stream, building a hill.
It was 1772. Nothing would change
but he changed it, who wouldn't see the beeches grown.
The manmade lakes overrun with reeds,

the little ruin more ruined than ever—
we'd take the folly first, the man beside me said,
in the crisp voice of retired officer,
Sunday painter, church organist.

All that summer he was bored.

Mrs. A: They say, Lady H____, that when good Americans die they go to Paris.

Lady H: Indeed? And when bad Americans die, where do they go to?

Lord L: Oh, they go to America.

—A Woman of No Importance

Memoirs of a Saint

after Magritte

I

Don't look at that cloud—
    it has breasts!
Don't say the word "breast"!

        I heard a voice
from the clouds. Though I walked
        through the valley

of the shadow of the breast hidden
        in the spelling lesson,
I feared the body. For neither the Virgin

        nor I, nor Sister Perpetua,
who found me sinfully lost in cloud,
        had breasts, I was sure.

If you were good—and I had been good,
        knowing no better—
you got a holy card: I had the one

        of a sexless blond
who had sprouted wings, quivering, huge,
        right through his clothes.

What did I want? The woman
        who held out a plate,
offering up her tortured eyes?

The man full of arrows
who wouldn't meet your gaze?
    O Sacred Heart,

you with the hole in your chest,
    the heart in flames,
the dainty hands, the curls—O Bearded Lady,

    pray for me.

2

O 1960! A cloud like a mushroom—
  don't talk about it.
Crawl out from under the desk.

    Even the President went to Mass.
Would go to Berlin to keep us safe.
    Would pronounce

what he'd been taught, the German
    for "I am a jelly doughnut."
His hair luffed in the wind of television.

    Six inches tall,
he was gray, dwarfed by the hand
    of my father,

who changed the channel, shooing us off.
    Enough!
You could never have enough missiles.

    His job was safe,
whatever it was he did in secret in the desert.
    He took off his dosimeter.

Far off in Brussels, in his dining room,
    the last Walloon master
wiped his brush. On canvas, an empty stage:

against the outer—
no, the inner—dark, a curtain of sky
turned back on itself.

Alone with the Alone at last,
Augustine looked down
on the mere girl who mouthed his prayer,

O give me
chastity and continents,
but not yet.

Eve at the Paradise

And then, the camera become too cruel,
        she appeared only in the flesh,
sewn into a clinging flesh-toned gown,
        nothing left

to the imagination, the breasts still high,
        the nipples boldly outlined
by a second skin of silk, the buttocks still firm.
        All this fashioned

from just a rib? Light years away on stage,
        how could she be older
than she looked? In the front row
        a man with binoculars

had to be chastened mid-song—
        "You'll kill me,"
she stage-whispered, which brought the house down.
        "Bury me in any old village,"

she'd say, "with a three-star restaurant."
        After a meal worth dying for,
tourists too young to know her name
        would pay a visit.

But for now, a clinic in Switzerland,
        a sheep in high meadow
awaiting the knife, the heart of the unborn lamb
        laid out on ice

about to be rushed to her bedside,
    that famous backside
awaiting the first injection—for now,
    she would almost sing,

her voice half angel's, half sin,
    wrapped in white fur.
She snarled, then purred a caress
    to the snake of a microphone.

One for the husband, at least in name,
    on a ranch somewhere out west.
One for my baby, one for the road.
    One for the audience.

Which animals mate for life? After the show
    a meal at midnight,
the steak almost raw under a moon
    as alone as she was,

insomniac, ravenous. Bed at last at dawn,
    to sleep till noon
in the arms of Nembutal. Oh, to escape
    the gate's enormous wings

at the school for girls, long since bombed
    in the second great war!
From over the wall, the sweet stench
    of fruit rotting unpicked

and a lone peacock's cry, girlish, torn,
    a name screamed,
over and over, from what was once
    the Zoological Garden.

The Zoo in the Rain
The Snow Leopard

Something bellowed.
No one manned the zoo's ticket window,
only from somewhere came an echo,
a cry lifted bodily over the fence.

And there was the keeper's little door
at the back of a cage. The well-scrubbed floor,
the animal just a furious blur.
Next door a giraffe somehow stretched *down*

to tongue the leaves shed by mere maples.
It was Sunday, church bells pealing
the birds of paradise from their painted perches.
A parrot asked again to be forgiven.

A floe of cement—no, a whole archipelago
had been poured for the polar bear
who gently snored, granting absolution.
Around the corner, the snow leopard lounged

on a concrete altar. His patient glare
left raw the sacrament of meat.
Flies in procession, vestments aglitter,
a penitent sparrow denying the cold—

the leopard looked prepared
to wait for his native blue sheep
to be broken like bread.
The world's highest mountains

were missing. On the edge of the Great Plains,
where was the hut selling tea for the climber,
bitter with salt and rancid yak butter?
Where was the prayer wheel spinning

for leopard and tracker alike,
for the goat bought in the village
for leopard bait? I turned the corner
like a page of *National Geographic*.

The Porcupine

A flip of a peacock's fan,
a flush of hummingbird's throat—
past all that male flash, a flock
of human mothers pushed a safari of strollers.

Down the slippery slope
of a wet Wednesday morning,
down to the Monkey House they rolled.
The capuchin born in captivity

would have to learn how the monk
its mother kept the Divine Hours.
First learn the ropes strung heavenward.
Then there was nitpicking to be done.

On this side of the fence,
mothers talked small talk to babies,
who made large-animal noises.
Wild geese hissed at anything that moved—

at two tom-turkeys who strutted,
feathers ruffled like frontier whores.
Big cats had slunk into the inner dark,
even the giant tortoise pulled in his head.

"Look up," the sign said,
the sign of the porcupine.
I looked to the rain. The rain said, *farther*.
Up the gray tree, as far as it could go,

lodged a double handful of prickles.
Who wouldn't come in out of the rain?
I, who would mother nothing,
bristled with rough motherly love.

The Overland Bus

Somewhere overland, west of the known world,
it was Thursday—no, Saturday, 1805.
Dried fish and roots for supper again,
for which Captain Clark gave small thanks
it wasn't dog. Then the first white man
to see these parts took up his pen,
even as the words ambushed him.
A number of Indians about us gazeing.
This day proved very worm and Sultery,
nothing killed   men complaining—

no, it was much later, at a bus stop
somewhere in Idaho. Where did the bus go?
I marked my place in the book. I didn't know.
Did the man who asked me inch closer?
He was a stranger in these parts, too,
he said, to make me feel better;
for was he not just out of jail,
his worldly goods in a trash bag beside him?
He was about to admit whatever he'd done,
or not—oh, would the last frontier
please hurry up and close?

I took the next bus, wherever it went.
Down Overland Avenue we made our passage,
the driver, her knitting, and I. Past the Red Sea—
no, Red Steer, she purled. Past Big Bun Drive In,
she knitted something warm, something *worm.*
The heaters *Sultered* through—was it March?
Lost in the land of the Great Wall Restaurant,

I was just a white woman on the high plains,
a block of salt left out in the weeds
for the cattle to lick on their way to slaughter.

It was Monday, Clark was sure.
All the Party have greatly the advantage of me,
as they all relish the flesh of the dogs,
Several of which we purchased of the nativs.
From the split timber that they found buried,
they took only what they needed
there in the emptiness he called *our neighborhood,*
on the day their hunters found nothing to kill.
We have made it a point not to take any thing
belonging to the Indians even their wood.
Signals flaring, flicking a tail of fumes,
the bus stopped on that last word.

The Laurel Tree by the River

Then she saw the waters. . . . "O father," she cried, "help me!" If you rivers
really have some divine powers, work some transformation, and destroy this
beauty that makes me please all too well." —OVID

I

The mountains, come down to water level;
the water, rising to meet the mud.
Ducks, mating in the muck
in the season of love—

all month I watched over my father
where he lay like the old river he was.
His mind meandered where it would,
braiding around me, whoever I was.

I stood there, rooted.
He doubled back to damn the daughter
cut off, the oxbow lake
who still owed him grandchildren.

Where was the river that used to bear
the gods of sun and tumbleweed
on its broad back,
one snag to another?

I hugged the muddy bank,
I, his daughter, the one
whose leaves grew leathery
and poisonous, the mountain laurel.

2

In the dry season,
the leaves grow careless,
drawing near the fire.
Where the traveler warmed himself last night,

the clearing has been left to smolder—
so a man would journey all this way
just to lay his hand to the trunk
of the tree I'd become.

To brush his lips against the bark
and claim he felt a heartbeat,
these leaves rustling in breeze
or betrayal. Something stood still.

The duck was stuck on her nest,
the drake nowhere to be seen,
now that she sat brooding.
How he had chased her once,

running over the water to nip at her neck.
Deep in the woods, a dog bayed
after something smaller and smaller,
crashing its way through the understory.

To the Snow

To the canyon that came so close
to touching me, I was nothing.
What good was a truck gearing down
to go up to the snow?

Still, the walls of rock held themselves
at arm's length to make room.
A narrow hall. That wallpaper,
lichen splattered on basalt . . .

a bedroom carved out around me—
snow, where had you gone,
taking the road with you?
Where was the door?

The creek had something to say
on this, but not to me.
To the rocks the meltwater tumbled,
to the willows that reddened

at each wet word,
the radio crackled and spat.
And still Willie Nelson sang
in a whiny fuzz.

The pines strained under the weight
of all the dumb sad songs made one.
Love gone to seed,
love buried under snow—

where was a snowbird to feed?
A flock of juncos flung itself
like a lost scarf over the last weeds.
Mist coming down the mountain

to meet someone halfway—
I took off a glove. I lay down
and played angel. The snow held on,
a body of water that wouldn't melt.

Snow, let go. It's late.
You are corn mush. You are cold.
Let me cover you with this white sheet.
No one will know.

Moss in the Hamptons

in memory of Howard Moss

I

I thought I knew something
about loneliness, but I was wrong.
I'd never been that far east before,
out where Long Island at last

looked like an island, not a suburb.
In the low light of cocktail hour,
in a lone deck chair from the *Queen Mary,*
Moss looked at his watch and lifted his glass

like an anchor—but first laid out a dog biscuit,
though he didn't have a dog—
and over the rolling lawn-to-be
sailed a rusty but neighborly setter.

The gardener would come tomorrow
to fill in the bare patches we admired,
being too far inland to see the ocean.
He'd never owned a house before.

He looked more like a tortoise than ever,
drawing back into the crevice of kitchen,
happily, from the cavernous living room.
The troublesome heart had yet to make itself felt.

2

I was just someone on the edge of the scene,
now as then, looking out a window,
leafing through a book—and there you are,
as young as I was then, on the lawn

in a photo of someone else's country house.
I don't recognize the others
or the island some afternoon after the war.
By a fraction of an inch you don't touch anything

but the grass, not even the blanket spread out.
I wanted to tell you there's a new book on Chekhov.
Dear Moss, to whom can I show it?
You're dead. Still, you'd like it.

He's not a hermit anymore.
An actress on each arm, more women in the wings,
he's with St. Ambrose, who counseled Augustine
never to go to parties in his hometown,

it would only bring him grief.
In a place like Yalta you might cough in peace.
I thought I knew about islands but I was wrong.
I'd never been so far east before.

There Now

He wasn't himself, your father.
Not even your mother could rouse him,
even to the old arguments.
So the toast was cold?

The room was cold where he burned,
at sea in their old bed,
like some small craft turned on its side,
spars bony under a clammy sail.

Six cigarettes a day the doctor allowed.
One burned, neglected, its bedside vigil
capsized into a mere breath of ash.
Your mother lit another.

His pale hands barely touched his pale food
as if already he were beyond all this,
although he'd not been told how ill he was.
Could he not have known?

Already he had the cast of a northern saint,
one so pale he still glows under the dust
that is the long history of forgetfulness.
One who holds a small building

like a baby forever toward us,
whose attentions soon turn elsewhere,
to love or lunch, the tarnished leaf
of grace falling but never touching us.

The ocean sinks into its salt
or we rise above it, the plane torn
between the gravity of human wishes
and cloud spun from airy nothing—

these white loaves, the whiter fish drifted
from the deep blue a miniaturist filled in
behind some unconvincing rocks,
floating a far-off frill of waves

stitched to a little gash of boat,
a saint left standing around, hands full,
looking cold and a little lost.
And then we, too, are above it all,

the earth bandaged with cotton wool.
There, your mother would say in promise
of great distance from a little crescent
of scar. *There now. There, there.*

The Dead of Summer

Each day whittled a little smaller,
each night dug a little deeper in the dark—
this is the season Aquinas must have loved,
not the heat so much as the humility.

Would an angel assume a body in this weather?
Why be in more than one place at once,
why not elsewhere altogether?
It's three a.m., still hot, not still—

how like the cicada may we praise
the cicada endlessly?
How may one creature move another?
On the lawn we lie, even the spirit dampened,

leaving the imprints of damp angels.
Does one angel illumine another?
Your parents' large sad house is dark,
a last firefly fitfully praising

the dark trail deeper into the dark.
Down by the boat in the trees
the obstinate ghost of your father wavers,
just a flicker of cigarette.

He doesn't want to come in.
What *does* an angel want, Thomas wanted to know.
Two fingers on the rocks, a drink to nurse?
Does the local distance slur angelic speech?

Stay where you are, the dead say, *don't get up.*
Does the angel ever forsake a man?
He walks his old unhappiness like the dog it is,
awaiting the ferry that no longer crosses the Sound.

Rain on rain has hollowed a fresh mound
until it's a boat of mud
in a flower-choked sea of graves.
How like him you look,

where you lie in the little light,
half dark, half salt. Under my hand,
under your dim skin, your dear skull.
My lips to your eyebrow kiss the bone below.

Head, Perhaps of an Angel

limestone, with traces of polychromy, c. 1250

Point Dume was the point,
he said, but we never came close,
no matter how far we walked the shale
        broken from California.

Someone's garden
had slipped, hanging itself by a vine
from the cliffs of some new Babylon
        past Malibu.

Drowning the words
the wind didn't fling back in our faces,
the Pacific washed up a shell:
        around an alabastron

of salt water for the dead,
seaweed rustled its papers, drying them out,
until it died. Waves kept crashing
        into the heart

of each shell
I held to my ear like a phone,
but they were just the waves of my blood.
        And through it all

I heard him say,
how could it be nine months ago
his grandson had taken his own life,
        somewhere back east?

He was fifteen.
O Pacific, what good is our grief?
Something screamed at the sandy child
who poured seawater

into a hole.
Child, you will never empty the ocean,
Augustine said. *How can I believe?*
The wet fist of a wave

dissolved in sand.
Like a saint, a seagull flapped down the beach
in search of something raw—an angel
with an empty pail?

No, a teenage boy,
hands as big as a man's, held a sea slug
quaking like an aspic. Under a rock, another one
drew into its body

a sea creature
larger than itself. *Live,* said Death,
to child and childless alike, indifferently.
I am coming.

In the provinces, rain is a diversion.
—EDMUND and JULES DE GONCOURT

Variante de la Tristesse: The Sadness of the Subtropics

after Magritte

Just off the highway to Starke,
    there was a trout
in the boatyard, as big as a boat.

    Low cloud in high water,
she floated, the air a body of water
    begging to be wrung out.

But I couldn't, for had I not fins by now?
    Your cold-blooded love,
your mermaid wrong way round,

    scales above the waist,
still woman below, I—but it doesn't matter
    now, does it?

Your hand warm under my skirt
    as we sailed,
just over the limit, past the trout,

    the car a grave
and private place—O my mammalian love,
    wasn't this world enough?

We would sit down, and think which way to walk.
    I by the tide would complain—
you'd kiss my foul, my fishy mouth—

Love, stop.
This wasn't about love. Vaster than engines
and more slow,

the trout curved in the currentless air.
O pink stripe of paint,
whose youthful hue sat on her skin

like mourning!
Worms shall try that long-preserved virginity.
An hundred years

should go to catch some silk-floss fly.
O Darling, Green Midge!
O Black Prince, Blue Professor!

Admiral of the Parking Lot

All alike we sail to a shore of lies,
        as Pindar said.
        But first a quick stop
at a Quik Mart somewhere in Florida;
        a man wanted something
        to dull the dullness of the road.
Out of love, I sat in the car and watched
        the gravel until it blurred.
        A map of New World islands,
each bean the chief laid out on the table
        in the white god's galley
        a lie in his own defense . . .

Against the gray gravel a red admiral flailed,
        a butterfly battling the air
        with stained-glass sails.
A prayer streaked red and black and white—
        Sunday in New Spain,
        Columbus wrote,
the natives would paint themselves,
        in their nakedness,
        as if with clothes.
I watched a man nearly his age
        on the first voyage—
        just twenty-something—
lay in provisions: *Playboy* and a Big Gulp.
        O Miss October! Nina!
        The earth is not round
but pear-shaped, with a nipple on top;

the Admiral was right.
Whoever swore belief
took a native woman into his berth.
And if she scratched at him,
a belt would remedy that.

O admiral of the parking lot,
tattered, down on your luck,
stunned by a truck! Your wings
lay open for king and queen to read.
In the Book of Privileges,
you wanted your string
of titles back, and the chain of islands
that went along with them.
You want to lead
one last crazed crusade to Jerusalem.
You want—forget Isabella.
She's dead. And the city of gold?
Forget Marco Polo and his millions,
the liar. No one lies better
than a poet.
Let me read to you while we wait
for history or immortality,
whichever takes you first.
Let others praise bright roads,
Horace began,
and praised them all.
O valiant men, who with me have often
suffered worse things,
drive out your cares with wine:
tomorrow once again we sail the Ocean Sea.

Persephone in the Underworld

Je suis comme le roi d'un pays pluvieux,
Riche, mais impuissant, jeune et pourtant très vieux
—BAUDELAIRE

Demeter in Florida

O the dank state of December!
Mother descended from the plane
to pronounce Florida excessively green.
Her coat stayed on. Her coat stayed brown.
The trees were much too tall—
she had to crane her neck to see the birds
making a racket even in the rain.
She hauled out binoculars
and looked at her long-lost daughter.
Distinguishing marks of a professor?
Dull plumage. Queen of the kingdom of decay?
She opened the field guide to the underworld.
A dead leaf inching down a tree trunk
turned out to be just a wren.
The wren screamed, "Teacher, teacher!"

What good were you to me, Mother,
who'd taught me what I knew of birds?
Where was the shade of Darwin,
who also ate bugs, to lecture the bird?
A column of ants marched down the walk
to where a French fry lay in ketchup.
The anole that looked like a fountain pen
ate the lot of them, as we, too, retired for lunch.

And so to the ivory tower, where we rode the elevator
to higher and higher office. And when it was over,
the goddess announced all she'd seen her daughter do
was move paper from one place to another.
The young man who'd dared to laugh at your thirst—
Mother, how did you turn him into a lizard?
Teach me, down to the spots on the tail.
I, who wasn't thinking of you
when I ate a few seeds of the pomegranate.

Footnote to Plato

The entire European philosophical tradition consists of a series of footnotes to Plato.   —ALFRED NORTH WHITEHEAD

I was queen of a rainy state, rich
in the trickle-down, the aftermath
of an afternoon thunder shower,
irony dripping for another hour.
A gallant anole laid down his pin stripes
over a puddle, that I might pass.
The squirrel learned his lesson at the college
of the trash can: the open book
of a hawk took him, to feed her young,
in front of the stone-faced library.

Inside, a young man, desperate
to narrow his search, dared raise his voice
to ask Plato's last name.
Are we amused, cicadas? You males drone on
about the tools of the court poet,
of Ralegh, that old pirate-philosopher—

am I cold-blooded, too, alligator?
I've heard you crossed the street,
the light being green,
to the natural history museum,
to see the jar in which you'll be curled,
next to the jar of eggs you laid, already culled.
Oh, bear me across the Styx

to the golf retirement village.
All night the dead male poets pace the measure
of words that went into the water hazard
where you, queen of the dead, hold court.

The Pelican

Because it amused the queen in me,
at the edge of the underworld
the fishermen fed the pelicans.
The splutter of motor meant food—
suddenly brown pelicans swarmed the dock.
In their scholars' robes, they begged.
They waddled. They clacked their empty bills
to show what they knew while, off to the side,
an old woman and her daughter, no longer young,
took a hammer to an oyster.

A mother wants the limp wet muscle for bait.
And a daughter she'd long ago taught
to scatter the shell they'd crushed
over the water to attract the fish.
The mother sat in her lawn chair.
It was only a matter of time—half a beer—
until the sheepshead took the hook.
It was an ugly fish, all head,
also called a teacher in those parts.

The Civil War

After great battles generally come great rains.
　　　　　　　　　—PLUTARCH

I will never forget that library in the rain,
that room relocked by the librarian
who let us in. She stabbed a pencil
into her hair; there was war to wage
against cockroach, termite, voracious reader—
what was the difference? None of us
could touch her books until we filled out her forms.

We sat a long time, waiting for history,
camped in our coats in the confederacy
of a rebel air conditioner.
And when a volume at length was brought,
a book louse had been there before me,
General Sherman clearing the way.
I was just rain come lately, turning one leaf
after another, and there rose the Old South,
a faint whiff of rot. A warehouse of sugar burning,
all the men's faces, but one, dark in the firelight—

all you could see out the window was rain.
We sat scribbling, barely whispering,
lest we draw fire. I won't forget
how a pillow was brought—but for someone else.
No, to cradle a book. If the hands were gloved,
the librarian of the dead
surrendered its pages to be turned.

Subtropical Elegy

for Hal Korn,
in memory of Amy Clampitt

Late One January

There at a fence in Florida
the three of us had stood, wet to the knee,
in weeds that were busy dying. From the other side
a few cattle stared as if made gods,

incurious even as they chewed.
Only the live oak moved. Did a bough start to break?
No, it held still for the cool,
wet winding-sheet of the breeze.

And, farther back in the afterworld,
sandhill cranes wintering there
ignored us even as they eased away.
Like the dead, they had no time for us.

I could believe in the next world
if it were just the other side
of that fence. The gray body
of bird made wing to dwell above us . . .

at the diorama in the museum you stood
in front of the crane, eye to glass eye,
your arm reflected against a long gray wing.
You lifted the receiver—I guess you'd call it that—

to talk to the bird-prisoner beyond the glass
and heard from the other side
the deathlike rattle, the raw ululation
hewn from the pine barrens of this world,

planed and sanded into a threnody.

September Vigil

through landscapes of untended memory
                    —The Kingfisher

A spider has spun from dust to dust.
Something is written down the web,
like your name, the *A* felled,
the *M* turned on its side in pain,

valley after valley in the shadow of the spider,
who wound its prey in silk.
Eternal light shines upon it as it eats.
Overhead a storm cell has spread.

Under the rakish black hat last March,
you were bald. The half-life of cobalt
just over five years—in six months you'd be
a handful of ash under a birch tree.

But, back then, irradiant, you'd talked of the house,
the first you'd ever owned, and at your age,
imagine. A Renaissance chair,
so the antique dealer claimed,

and Hal insisting you should have it,
there, by the window, by the birch.
Tea shivered in its thick cup. Under New York,
the subway burrowed deep in the underworld.

West of Last Winter

a kingfisher's burnished plunge, the color of felicity afire
—The Kingfisher

Dead woman, did I tell you how I stood
in the hardware store, and couldn't tell you why?
A packet of love-lies-bleeding seed?
A dead-bolt to keep you—was it *in* or *out?*

Nails were served up like the clay feast
the Egyptians entombed with the dead,
lest one go hungry in the afterlife.
And there, a tender fresh-cut length of rope.

Between the upper- and the underworld,
a stuffed goose hung, wings extended forever,
tips almost singed by the ceiling lights.
A mounted moose-head looked on, lachrymose.

The goose flew straight for the wall of feathers.
Dearest was the kingfisher's skin
laid open like a map, the head turned to the side
as if in sleep,

the skin of a small country
that hovered on the chafe of wings,
the borders sealed,
feathers a blue-green flame.

South of September

down on down, the uninhabitable sorrow
                    —The Kingfisher

The heat rising in dizzy columns—
in the upper world it was a good day
to rise above all this, to be a vulture
come to clean the bones of the dead.

The death's-head moth in tatters in the parking lot.
The robin, soft under the wheel.
The owl that my student scraped up where it fell,
nearly weightless, the claw still clenched,

all that wing useless—I could believe in the soul
if it were the gecko on the window, drawn by hunger
to lamplight, a creature so pale you could see
the heart go black, the blue lungs fill.

At last, out of exhaustion, I thought,
the leaves of the live oak would have to fall.
What made it happen, I asked my brother the botanist.
He said, the holdfast lets go.

He was wrong about everything but seaweed,
the holdfast letting the rock stay,
letting it go. *In her sleep,*
the voice on the phone said.

We would not have you ignorant, I read,
concerning those who are asleep,
lest you grieve. A handful of ash
under leaves fallen from a northern birch.

The Eden of Florida

As if lying in the mud
waiting for the blood to move
could be called *thinking*,
God the alligator had second thoughts.

About dry land
and the creatures who stalked it—
half in the sinkhole, half out,
the alligator looked on all he'd made,

looking for food.
His was the slowest yawn ever,
the unmoved mover
falling asleep, waiting for it to be over.

The eyelid of stone fluttered,
and then the great jaw drifted down.
Back into the black muck
of omniscience the godhead settled.

Of what had I tasted?
Who drew that ragged breath but I,
the higher animal,
fallen from grace onto an ant hill?

I was the only one in clothes.
A big blond hawk took the bones of a bird
out of thin air
back to the empty nest of heaven.

The rusty hinge
of a butterfly stuck, then staggered
        into the New World.
As if a breviary had fallen open to the day

        the swamp was taken
in the name of a god not alligator
        but made in our likeness,
upright, snappish, one who ate flesh.

About the Author

Debora Greger is the author of five previous books of poems, *Movable Islands, And, The 1002nd Night, Off-Season at the Edge of the World,* and *Desert Fathers, Uranium Daughters.* She has won, among other honors, the Grolier Prize, the Discovery/*The Nation* Award, the Peter I. B. Lavan Younger Poets Award, an Award in Literature from the American Academy and Institute of Arts and Letters, and the Brandeis University Award in Poetry. She has received the Amy Lowell Poetry Traveling Scholarship and grants from the Ingram Merrill Foundation, the Guggenheim Foundation, and the National Endowment for the Arts. Ms. Greger teaches at the University of Florida, and she lives in Florida and England.